INTRODUCTION

'do good...
and re[...]

Do you ever wish the world could be a better place? Do you think that if only people could be more caring, more generous, less selfish, more loving, that the world we live in would be so different? Mahatma Gandhi, an inspirational leader in India in the early part of the 20th century, once said, 'Be the change you want to see in the world.' What he meant is that if we want the world to be a better place, each one of us has to change it ourselves, one action at a time. Why not start this Lent?

From Shrove Tuesday (Pancake Day) to Easter Day there is an action for you to do on six days in each week of Lent. Lent is 40 days long to match the amount of time that Jesus spent in the wilderness. Sundays are not counted because every Sunday is a reminder of Easter Day.

The actions are quite simple. What makes them challenging is how you do them and, if we all do them, then the world really could become the place that God wants it to be: one person at a time, one action at a time.

This Lent start a revolution –
and be the change you want
to see!

**Paula Gooder &
Peter Babington**

SHROVE TUESDAY

CELEBRATE MORE ☐

Have a pancake party

ASH WEDNESDAY

SAY SORRY ☐

Think about something you have done wrong and say sorry for it.

THURSDAY

BE MORE GIVING ☐

Get a jar and put your small change into it each day. At the end of Lent give to a charity.

FRIDAY CARE FOR THOSE IN NEED ☐

Watch the news. Pray for someone or something you've seen on it.

SATURDAY

ENJOY OUR WORLD ☐

Plant some seeds and care for them as they grow.

SEED
Seed Type:
Date Collected:
Collected From:
Collected By:

MONDAY BE MORE CREATIVE ☐

Make something today,
like a cake, a picture,
a model, a poem
or a story.

TUESDAY CARE FOR THE WORLD ☐

Turn off
the lights
in rooms
that no one
is using.

WEDNESDAY BE MORE LOVING ☐

Tell someone you love them.

THURSDAY BE MORE CURIOUS ☐

Think of a question you've always wanted to know the answer to and see if you can find it out.

FRIDAY BE MORE GRATEFUL ☐

Say thank you to someone for who they are or what they do.

Thank You :)

SATURDAY NOTICE THE WORLD AROUND YOU ☐

Walk somewhere today and notice the things around you – birds singing, sun shining or rain splashing!

MONDAY BE MORE THANKFUL ☐

Say thank you to God for one of your meals today.

TUESDAY
BE MORE FRIENDLY ☐

Play with someone you don't normally play with.

WEDNESDAY
BE MORE GENEROUS ☐

Give a small present to someone you know.

THURSDAY

MAKE YOUR LOCAL AREA CLEANER ☐

Fill a bag with litter

(then put it all in the bin!)

FRIDAY — DO SOMETHING DIFFERENT ☐

Have a TV/computer game-free day and do something different instead.

SATURDAY

KEEP IN TOUCH MORE ☐

Phone someone you love but haven't seen for a while.

MONDAY TAKE CARE OF YOUR HOME ☐

Tidy a room or a cupboard in your house.

TUESDAY BE MORE OPEN ☐

Try something new, for example a different food or a new experience.

WEDNESDAY
BE A GOOD NEIGHBOUR ☐

Say hi to your neighbours today or when you next see them.

THURSDAY BE MORE PEACEFUL ☐

Listen to a piece of music that makes you feel relaxed.

FRIDAY HAVE MORE FUN ☐

Take time to play a game with someone.

SATURDAY THINK OF OTHERS MORE ☐

Do a job that someone else normally does, like the washing-up or taking the rubbish out.

MONDAY SAVE WATER ☐

Use the washing-
up water to wate
some plants.

TUESDAY

**CARE FOR YOUR
FRIENDS MORE** ☐

Make a list of your
friends' birthdays
and remember to
send them birthday cards.

WEDNESDAY

LISTEN MORE CAREFULLY ☐

Ask someone how
they are and take
time to listen
to the answer.

THURSDAY
SLOW DOWN ☐
Take longer
over breakfast
and really taste
your cornflakes
(or whatever else you have!)

FRIDAY — THINK MORE POSITIVELY ☐
Make a list of all
the good things in
your life and thank
God for them.

SATURDAY
SHARE MORE ☐
Make some cakes
and share them
with your friends.

Week 6

MONDAY BE STILL ☐

Sit still for five minutes and listen to your breathing.

TUESDAY
BE MORE WELCOMING ☐

Invite a friend to tea.

WEDNESDAY BE MORE THOUGHTFUL ☐

Think about what might make someone you know happy, then do it!

THURSDAY
SMILE MORE ☐
Give lots of smiles way today.

FRIDAY BE AWARE OF OTHERS ☐
Make a list of up to five people you have met today, and then pray for them.

SATURDAY
LIVE MORE SIMPLY ☐
Find something you don't use and give it away.

GREAT

GOOD JOB

WEL'

MONDAY BE MORE ENCOURAGING ☐
Say kind things to people you meet today, like 'well done', 'good job', 'great'

TUESDAY REMEMBER MORE ☐
Learn the words of something by heart, for example a poem, a prayer or a song.

WEDNESDAY
BE MORE IMAGINATIVE
Find out what someone has give up for Lent – and buy it for them as an Easter present

THURSDAY

LOVE ONE ANOTHER ☐

f the seeds you planted
have grown enough,
give some away.
If not, buy a plant
or some flowers
for someone.

FRIDAY THINK ABOUT THE GOOD FRIDAY STORY ☐

Make an Easter Garden.

(For tips on how to do this, see the
LLLL website – www.livelent.net)

SATURDAY

SHARE THE EASTER STORY ☐

Give someone
an Easter card
ven better, make it first!)

TO PARENTS AND CARERS ...

Have a look through the booklet before your child star to do the actions so you know what is involved.

The actions are aimed primarily at school-age children Help your child to do any actions that they are finding difficult or don't understand. You may need to interpret some of the actions creatively to make them suitable fo your child's ability.

Identify any actions that you need to be involved in wit your child and make sure your child knows what they must ask you before they do them.

Remind your child that they must not do anything outside of school or home or talk to anyone they do no know unless you are with them – it is important that they are safe while doing the actions.

Some of the actions involve accessing web sites – as for all internet use, make sure that your children are accessing web sites safely and with supervision.

There are instructions and extra help for actions indicated with an asterisk (*) on the supporting web site, www.livelent.net. You'll also find other supporting resources there. Pay us a visit.